# Mindfulness Journal

# Mindfulness
# Journal

—

## Be present with
## your thoughts
## every day

Emma Van Hinsbergh

SIRIUS

**SIRIUS**

This edition published in 2022 by Sirius Publishing, a division of
Arcturus Publishing Limited,
26/27 Bickels Yard, 151–153 Bermondsey Street,
London SE1 3HA

ISBN: 978-1-3988-2135-4
AD010657NT

Printed in China

# INTRODUCTION

## What is mindfulness?

Mindfulness is a gentle form of meditation that helps you to focus on the moment and develop a greater perspective on life. Being mindful helps you to appreciate the small things in life and to become fully engaged in activities. Above all, mindfulness is about being kind and forgiving towards yourself. By focusing on the present, you can banish negative internal chatter and learn to accept whatever feelings or emotions arise in your awareness at each moment.

Research shows it has a host of health benefits such as relieving stress, treating heart disease, lowering blood pressure, reducing chronic pain, improving sleep, and alleviating gut issues. It can also help to improve mental wellbeing and has been used to treat depression, eating disorders, anxiety, and addiction issues.

## DIY techniques

There are several ways to build a mindfulness habit.

- Find a quiet spot and focus on your breathing or on a word or "mantra" that you repeat silently, while allowing your thoughts to come and go without judgment.

- Start a steady and relaxed naming of emotions such anger, joy, or irritation. Accept these feelings without judgment and let them go.
- Notice each part of your body in succession from head to toe, paying attention to any sensations such as itching or tingling.
- Pay attention to sensory triggers such as sights, sounds, touches, tastes, and smells.

The beauty of mindfulness is that you can easily incorporate it into your daily routine and, unlike many forms of meditation, it doesn't have to involve putting life on hold for hours on end. Focusing your attention on the sensations you feel as you brush your teeth, go for a walk, or eat a piece of fruit is a great way to be in the moment and to reap the benefits.

The effect of mindfulness tends to increase with time so try to build in at least 20 minutes a day if you can.

Use this handy journal to help you appreciate daily moments of joy and gratitude and to achieve a state of focused relaxation by deliberately paying attention to your thoughts and sensations without any sort of judgment. If your mind wanders into planning, daydreaming, or criticism, notice where it has gone and gently redirect it to sensations in the present.

From setting a morning intention and harnessing the energy of nature, to switching off your phone and focusing on your breathing, this beautifully illustrated book will help you to be fully present and aware of the precious moments in your life on a daily basis.

# Morning

Date ___ / ___ / ___

My intention today is...

.........................................................................

.........................................................................

.........................................................................

.........................................................................

I will
take time to
focus on...

.........................................................

.........................................................

.........................................................

.........................................................

## DIGITAL DETOX

I will turn off all my phones, tablets, and

computers for.................................................minutes.

My positive affirmation will be ...

.........................................................................................

.........................................................................................

## NATURAL HEALING

I will harness nature's energy by...

.........................................................................................

.........................................................................................

.........................................................................................

.........................................................................................

## HAPPINESS MANTRA

Today I felt gratitude for...

...............................................................

...............................................................

...............................................................

> *I closed my eyes to focus on my breath, in and out, for a few minutes. These thoughts came to my mind...*
>
> ...........................................
>
> ...........................................
>
> ...........................................
>
> ...........................................
>
> ...........................................

## DAILY MINDFULNESS

One thing I learned today was...

...............................................................

...............................................................

...............................................................

The most beautiful thing today was...

...............................................................

...............................................................

...............................................................

...............................................................

 # Morning

Date ___ / ___ / ___

My intention today is...

..................................................................................................

..................................................................................................

..................................................................................................

..................................................................................................

I will
take time to
focus on...

..................................................................

..................................................................

..................................................................

..................................................................

## DIGITAL DETOX

I will turn off all my phones, tablets, and

computers for.................................................minutes.

My positive affirmation will be ...

..................................................................................................

..................................................................................................

## NATURAL HEALING

I will harness nature's energy by...

..................................................................................................

..................................................................................................

..................................................................................................

..................................................................................................

# Evening

## HAPPINESS MANTRA

Today I felt gratitude for...

........................................................................

........................................................................

........................................................................

........................................................................

> *I closed my eyes to focus on my breath, in and out, for a few minutes. These thoughts came to my mind...*
>
> ........................................................
>
> ........................................................
>
> ........................................................
>
> ........................................................
>
> ........................................................

## DAILY MINDFULNESS

One thing I learned today was...

........................................................................

........................................................................

........................................................................

........................................................................

The most beautiful thing today was...

........................................................................

........................................................................

........................................................................

........................................................................

# Morning

Date ___ / ___ / ___

My intention today is...

.......................................................................................

.......................................................................................

.......................................................................................

.......................................................................................

I will
take time to
focus on...

.......................................................................

.......................................................................

.......................................................................

.......................................................................

## DIGITAL DETOX

I will turn off all my phones, tablets, and

computers for.................................................minutes.

My positive affirmation will be ...

.........................................................................................................................

.........................................................................................................................

## NATURAL HEALING

I will harness nature's energy by...

.........................................................................................................................

.........................................................................................................................

.........................................................................................................................

# Evening

## HAPPINESS MANTRA

Today I felt gratitude for...

........................................................................

........................................................................

........................................................................

........................................................................

*I closed my eyes to focus on my breath, in and out, for a few minutes. These thoughts came to my mind...*

........................................................................

........................................................................

........................................................................

........................................................................

........................................................................

## DAILY MINDFULNESS

One thing I learned today was...

........................................................................

........................................................................

........................................................................

........................................................................

The most beautiful thing today was...

........................................................................

........................................................................

........................................................................

........................................................................

# Morning

My intention today is...

.................................................................................................

.................................................................................................

.................................................................................................

.................................................................................................

I will
take time to
focus on...

.................................................................

.................................................................

.................................................................

.................................................................

## DIGITAL DETOX

I will turn off all my phones, tablets, and

computers for.................................................minutes.

My positive affirmation will be ...

.................................................................................................

.................................................................................................

## NATURAL HEALING

I will harness nature's energy by...

.................................................................................................

.................................................................................................

.................................................................................................

.................................................................................................

# Evening

## HAPPINESS MANTRA

Today I felt gratitude for...

........................................................

........................................................

........................................................

........................................................

*I closed my eyes to focus on my breath, in and out, for a few minutes. These thoughts came to my mind...*

........................................................

........................................................

........................................................

........................................................

........................................................

## DAILY MINDFULNESS

One thing I learned today was...

........................................................................................

........................................................................................

........................................................................................

........................................................................................

The most beautiful thing today was...

........................................................................................

........................................................................................

........................................................................................

........................................................................................

# Morning

Date ___ / ___ / ___

My intention today is...

........................................................

........................................................

........................................................

........................................................

I will
take time to
focus on...

........................................................

........................................................

........................................................

........................................................

## DIGITAL DETOX

I will turn off all my phones, tablets, and

computers for................................................minutes.

My positive affirmation will be ...

........................................................

........................................................

## NATURAL HEALING

I will harness nature's energy by...

........................................................

........................................................

........................................................

........................................................

# Evening

## HAPPINESS MANTRA

Today I felt gratitude for...

.................................................................................

.................................................................................

.................................................................................

.................................................................................

> *I closed my eyes to focus on my breath, in and out, for a few minutes. These thoughts came to my mind...*
>
> .................................................
>
> .................................................
>
> .................................................
>
> .................................................
>
> .................................................

## DAILY MINDFULNESS

One thing I learned today was...

.................................................................................

.................................................................................

.................................................................................

.................................................................................

The most beautiful thing today was...

.................................................................................

.................................................................................

.................................................................................

.................................................................................

 # Morning

Date ___ / ___ / ___

My intention today is...

.......................................................................................................

.......................................................................................................

.......................................................................................................

.......................................................................................................

I will
take time to
focus on...

....................................................

....................................................

....................................................

....................................................

## DIGITAL DETOX

I will turn off all my phones, tablets, and

computers for.................................................minutes.

My positive affirmation will be ...

.......................................................................................................

.......................................................................................................

## NATURAL HEALING

I will harness nature's energy by...

.......................................................................................................

.......................................................................................................

.......................................................................................................

# Evening

## HAPPINESS MANTRA

Today I felt gratitude for...

.......................................................................................

.......................................................................................

.......................................................................................

*I closed my eyes to focus on my breath, in and out, for a few minutes. These thoughts came to my mind...*

.......................................................

.......................................................

.......................................................

.......................................................

.......................................................

## DAILY MINDFULNESS

One thing I learned today was...

.......................................................................................................................

.......................................................................................................................

.......................................................................................................................

.......................................................................................................................

The most beautiful thing today was...

.......................................................................................................................

.......................................................................................................................

.......................................................................................................................

.......................................................................................................................

 # Morning

Date ___ / ___ / ___

My intention today is...

.................................................................

.................................................................

.................................................................

.................................................................

I will
take time to
focus on...

.................................................

.................................................

.................................................

.................................................

## DIGITAL DETOX

I will turn off all my phones, tablets, and

computers for..............................................minutes.

My positive affirmation will be ...

.................................................................................

.................................................................................

## NATURAL HEALING

I will harness nature's energy by...

.................................................................................

.................................................................................

.................................................................................

.................................................................................

## HAPPINESS MANTRA

Today I felt gratitude for...

....................................................

....................................................

....................................................

*I closed my eyes to focus on my breath, in and out, for a few minutes. These thoughts came to my mind...*

....................................................

....................................................

....................................................

....................................................

## DAILY MINDFULNESS

One thing I learned today was...

....................................................

....................................................

....................................................

....................................................

The most beautiful thing today was...

....................................................

....................................................

....................................................

....................................................

# Morning

Date ___ / ___ / ___

My intention today is...

.................................................................................

.................................................................................

.................................................................................

.................................................................................

I will
take time to
focus on...

.................................................................

.................................................................

.................................................................

.................................................................

## DIGITAL DETOX

I will turn off all my phones, tablets, and

computers for.................................................minutes.

My positive affirmation will be ...

.................................................................................................

.................................................................................................

## NATURAL HEALING

I will harness nature's energy by...

.................................................................................................

.................................................................................................

.................................................................................................

.................................................................................................

# Evening

## HAPPINESS MANTRA

Today I felt gratitude for...

........................................................................

........................................................................

........................................................................

*I closed my eyes to focus on my breath, in and out, for a few minutes. These thoughts came to my mind...*

........................................................................

........................................................................

........................................................................

........................................................................

........................................................................

## DAILY MINDFULNESS

One thing I learned today was...

........................................................................

........................................................................

........................................................................

........................................................................

The most beautiful thing today was...

........................................................................

........................................................................

........................................................................

........................................................................

 **Morning**

Date ___ / ___ / ___

My intention today is...

........................................................................................

........................................................................................

........................................................................................

........................................................................................

I will
take time to
focus on...

........................................................

........................................................

........................................................

........................................................

**DIGITAL DETOX**

I will turn off all my phones, tablets, and

computers for.........................................................minutes.

My positive affirmation will be ...

........................................................................................

........................................................................................

**NATURAL HEALING**

I will harness nature's energy by...

........................................................................................

........................................................................................

........................................................................................

........................................................................................

# Evening

## HAPPINESS MANTRA

Today I felt gratitude for...

...........................................................................

...........................................................................

...........................................................................

*I closed my eyes to focus on my breath, in and out, for a few minutes. These thoughts came to my mind...*

...........................................................

...........................................................

...........................................................

...........................................................

...........................................................

## DAILY MINDFULNESS

One thing I learned today was...

...........................................................................................

...........................................................................................

...........................................................................................

...........................................................................................

The most beautiful thing today was...

...........................................................................................

...........................................................................................

...........................................................................................

...........................................................................................

 # Morning

My intention today is...

.........................................................................

.........................................................................

.........................................................................

.........................................................................

I will
take time to
focus on...

.........................................................

.........................................................

.........................................................

.........................................................

## DIGITAL DETOX

I will turn off all my phones, tablets, and

computers for.............................................minutes.

My positive affirmation will be ...

.........................................................................

.........................................................................

## NATURAL HEALING

I will harness nature's energy by...

.........................................................................

.........................................................................

.........................................................................

# Evening

## HAPPINESS MANTRA

Today I felt gratitude for...

.................................................................

.................................................................

.................................................................

> *I closed my eyes to focus on my breath, in and out, for a few minutes. These thoughts came to my mind...*
>
> .................................
>
> .................................
>
> .................................
>
> .................................
>
> .................................

## DAILY MINDFULNESS

One thing I learned today was...

.................................................................

.................................................................

.................................................................

.................................................................

The most beautiful thing today was...

.................................................................

.................................................................

.................................................................

.................................................................

 # Morning

Date ___ / ___ / ___

My intention today is...

..........................................................................................

..........................................................................................

..........................................................................................

..........................................................................................

I will
take time to
focus on...

..........................................................................................

..........................................................................................

..........................................................................................

..........................................................................................

## DIGITAL DETOX

I will turn off all my phones, tablets, and

computers for................................................minutes.

My positive affirmation will be ...

..........................................................................................

..........................................................................................

## NATURAL HEALING

I will harness nature's energy by...

..........................................................................................

..........................................................................................

..........................................................................................

..........................................................................................

## HAPPINESS MANTRA

Today I felt gratitude for...

..................................................................................

..................................................................................

..................................................................................

..................................................................................

*I closed my eyes to focus on my breath, in and out, for a few minutes. These thoughts came to my mind...*

..........................................

..........................................

..........................................

..........................................

..........................................

## DAILY MINDFULNESS

One thing I learned today was...

..................................................................................

..................................................................................

..................................................................................

..................................................................................

The most beautiful thing today was...

..................................................................................

..................................................................................

..................................................................................

..................................................................................

# Morning

My intention today is...

.................................................................................

.................................................................................

.................................................................................

.................................................................................

I will
take time to
focus on...

.................................................

.................................................

.................................................

.................................................

## DIGITAL DETOX

I will turn off all my phones, tablets, and

computers for.................................................minutes.

My positive affirmation will be ...

.................................................................................................

.................................................................................................

## NATURAL HEALING

I will harness nature's energy by...

.................................................................................................

.................................................................................................

.................................................................................................

.................................................................................................

# Evening

HAPPINESS MANTRA

Today I felt gratitude for...

.................................................................................................

.................................................................................................

.................................................................................................

.................................................................................................

*I closed my eyes to focus on my breath, in and out, for a few minutes. These thoughts came to my mind...*

.................................................................

.................................................................

.................................................................

.................................................................

.................................................................

DAILY MINDFULNESS

One thing I learned today was...

.................................................................................................

.................................................................................................

.................................................................................................

.................................................................................................

The most beautiful thing today was...

.................................................................................................

.................................................................................................

.................................................................................................

.................................................................................................

# Morning

Date ___ / ___ / ___

My intention today is...

.............................................................................

.............................................................................

.............................................................................

.............................................................................

## DIGITAL DETOX

I will turn off all my phones, tablets, and computers for...........................minutes.

My positive affirmation will be...

.............................................................................

.............................................................................

.............................................................................

I will take time
to focus on...

.............................................

.............................................

.............................................

.............................................

## NATURAL HEALING

I will harness nature's energy by...

.............................................................................

.............................................................................

.............................................................................

.............................................

# Evening

## HAPPINESS MANTRA

Today I felt gratitude for...

.................................................................................................................

.................................................................................................................

.................................................................................................................

## EVENING MEDITATIONS

One thing I learned today was...

.....................................................................................

.....................................................................................

.....................................................................................

.....................................................................................

*I closed my eyes to focus on my breath, in and out, for a few minutes. These thoughts came to my mind...*

...............................................

...............................................

...............................................

The most beautiful thing today was...

.................................................................................................

.................................................................................................................

.................................................................................................................

.................................................................................................................

.................................................................................................................

# Morning

Date ___ / ___ / ___

My intention today is...

......................................................................................................

......................................................................................................

......................................................................................................

......................................................................................................

## DIGITAL DETOX

I will turn off all my phones, tablets, and computers for.................................minutes.

My positive affirmation will be...

......................................................................................................

......................................................................................................

I will take time
to focus on...

...................................

...................................

...................................

...................................

## NATURAL HEALING

I will harness nature's energy by...

......................................................................................................

......................................................................................................

......................................................................................................

......................................................................................................

# Evening

## HAPPINESS MANTRA

Today I felt gratitude for...

.......................................................................................................................

.......................................................................................................................

.......................................................................................................................

## EVENING MEDITATIONS

One thing I learned today was...

.......................................................................................................................

.......................................................................................................................

.......................................................................................................................

.......................................................................................................................

*I closed my eyes to focus on my breath, in and out, for a few minutes. These thoughts came to my mind...*

.......................................................................

.......................................................................

.......................................................................

The most beautiful thing today was...

.......................................................................................................................

.......................................................................................................................

.......................................................................................................................

.......................................................................................................................

.......................................................................................................................

# Morning

Date ___ / ___ / ___

My intention today is...

...................................................................................................

...................................................................................................

...................................................................................................

...................................................................................................

### DIGITAL DETOX

I will turn off all my phones, tablets, and computers for.................................minutes.

My positive affirmation will be...

...................................................................................................

...................................................................................................

...................................................................................................

I will take time
to focus on...

.....................................

.....................................

.....................................

.....................................

### NATURAL HEALING

I will harness nature's energy by...

...................................................................................................

...................................................................................................

...................................................................................................

...................................................................................................

# Evening

## HAPPINESS MANTRA

Today I felt gratitude for...

........................................................................................................................................

........................................................................................................................................

........................................................................................................................................

## EVENING MEDITATIONS

One thing I learned today was...

........................................................................................................................................

........................................................................................................................................

........................................................................................................................................

........................................................................................................................................

*I closed my eyes to focus on my breath, in and out, for a few minutes. These thoughts came to my mind...*

........................................................................................................................................

........................................................................................................................................

........................................................................................................................................

The most beautiful thing today was...

........................................................................................................................................

........................................................................................................................................

........................................................................................................................................

........................................................................................................................................

# Morning

My intention today is...

.............................................................................................

.............................................................................................

.............................................................................................

.............................................................................................

## DIGITAL DETOX

I will turn off all my phones, tablets, and computers for..................................minutes.

My positive affirmation will be...

.............................................................................................

.............................................................................................

.............................................................................................

I will take time
to focus on...

...........................

...........................

...........................

...........................

## NATURAL HEALING

I will harness nature's energy by...

.............................................................................................

.............................................................................................

.............................................................................................

# Evening

## HAPPINESS MANTRA

Today I felt gratitude for...

.............................................................................................

.............................................................................................

.............................................................................................

## EVENING MEDITATIONS

One thing I learned today was...

.............................................................................................

.............................................................................................

.............................................................................................

.............................................................................................

*I closed my eyes to focus on my breath, in and out, for a few minutes. These thoughts came to my mind...*

.............................................................................................

.............................................................................................

.............................................................................................

The most beautiful thing today was...

.............................................................................................

.............................................................................................

.............................................................................................

.............................................................................................

.............................................................................................

# Morning

Date ___ / ___ / ___

My intention today is...

.............................................................................................................

.............................................................................................................

.............................................................................................................

.............................................................................................................

## DIGITAL DETOX

I will turn off all my phones, tablets, and computers for......................minutes.

My positive affirmation will be...

.............................................................................................................

.............................................................................................................

.............................................................................................................

I will take time
to focus on...

.........................................

.........................................

.........................................

.........................................

## NATURAL HEALING

I will harness nature's energy by...

.............................................................................................................

.............................................................................................................

.............................................................................................................

# Evening

## HAPPINESS MANTRA

Today I felt gratitude for...

........................................................................................................

........................................................................................................

........................................................................................................

## EVENING MEDITATIONS

One thing I learned today was...

........................................................................................................

........................................................................................................

........................................................................................................

........................................................................................................

*I closed my eyes to focus on my breath, in and out, for a few minutes. These thoughts came to my mind...*

........................................................

........................................................

........................................................

The most beautiful thing today was...

........................................................................................................

........................................................................................................

........................................................................................................

........................................................................................................

........................................................................................................

# Morning

Date ___ / ___ / ___

My intention today is...

.......................................................................................

.......................................................................................

.......................................................................................

.......................................................................................

## DIGITAL DETOX

I will turn off all my phones, tablets, and computers for.............................minutes.

My positive affirmation will be...

.......................................................................................

.......................................................................................

.......................................................................................

I will take time
to focus on...

.............................................

.............................................

.............................................

.............................................

## NATURAL HEALING

I will harness nature's energy by...

.......................................................................................

.......................................................................................

.......................................................................................

.......................................................................................

# Evening

## HAPPINESS MANTRA

Today I felt gratitude for...

.................................................................................................................

.................................................................................................................

.................................................................................................................

## EVENING MEDITATIONS

One thing I learned today was...

.................................................................................................

.................................................................................................

.................................................................................

*I closed my eyes to focus on my breath, in and out, for a few minutes. These thoughts came to my mind...*

..........................................

..........................................

..........................................

The most beautiful thing today was...

.................................................................................

.................................................................................................................

.................................................................................................................

.................................................................................................................

.................................................................................................................

# Morning

Date ___ / ___ / ___

My intention today is...

...........................................................................................

...........................................................................................

...........................................................................................

...........................................................................................

## DIGITAL DETOX

I will turn off all my phones, tablets, and computers for.................................minutes.

My positive affirmation will be...

...........................................................................................

...........................................................................................

...........................................................................................

I will take time
to focus on...

..............................................

..............................................

..............................................

..............................................

## NATURAL HEALING

I will harness nature's energy by...

...........................................................................................

...........................................................................................

...........................................................................................

# Evening

## HAPPINESS MANTRA

Today I felt gratitude for...

........................................................................................

........................................................................................

........................................................................................

## EVENING MEDITATIONS

One thing I learned today was...

........................................................................................

........................................................................................

........................................................................................

*I closed my eyes to focus on my breath, in and out, for a few minutes. These thoughts came to my mind...*

........................................................

........................................................

........................................................

The most beautiful thing today was...

........................................................................................

........................................................................................

........................................................................................

........................................................................................

# Morning

Date ___ / ___ / ___

My intention today is...

.................................................................................................

.................................................................................................

.................................................................................................

.................................................................................................

## DIGITAL DETOX

I will turn off all my phones, tablets, and computers for.............................minutes.

My positive affirmation will be...

.................................................................................................

.................................................................................................

.................................................................................................

I will take time
to focus on...

.................................................

.................................................

.................................................

.................................................

## NATURAL HEALING

I will harness nature's energy by...

.................................................................................................

.................................................................................................

.................................................................................................

# Evening

## HAPPINESS MANTRA

Today I felt gratitude for...

.................................................................................................

.................................................................................................

.................................................................................................

## EVENING MEDITATIONS

One thing I learned today was...

.................................................................................................

.................................................................................................

.................................................................................................

.................................................................................................

*I closed my eyes to focus on my breath, in and out, for a few minutes. These thoughts came to my mind...*

.........................................

.........................................

.........................................

The most beautiful thing today was...

.................................................................................................

.................................................................................................

.................................................................................................

.................................................................................................

# Morning

Date ___ / ___ / ___

My intention today is...

................................................................................................

................................................................................................

................................................................................................

................................................................................................

## DIGITAL DETOX

I will turn off all my phones, tablets, and computers for..............................minutes.

My positive affirmation will be...

................................................................................................

................................................................................................

................................................................................................

I will take time
to focus on...

..................................

..................................

..................................

..................................

## NATURAL HEALING

I will harness nature's energy by...

................................................................................................

................................................................................................

................................................................................................

# Evening

## HAPPINESS MANTRA

Today I felt gratitude for...

........................................................................................

........................................................................................

........................................................................................

## EVENING MEDITATIONS

One thing I learned today was...

........................................................................................

........................................................................................

........................................................................................

........................................................................................

*I closed my eyes to focus on my breath, in and out, for a few minutes. These thoughts came to my mind...*

........................................................................................

........................................................................................

........................................................................................

The most beautiful thing today was...

........................................................................................

........................................................................................

........................................................................................

........................................................................................

........................................................................................

# Morning

Date ___ / ___ / ___

My intention today is...

.................................................................................

.................................................................................

.................................................................................

.................................................................................

## DIGITAL DETOX

I will turn off all my phones, tablets, and computers for............................minutes.

My positive affirmation will be...

.................................................................................

.................................................................................

I will take time
to focus on...

...........................

...........................

...........................

...........................

## NATURAL HEALING

I will harness nature's energy by...

.................................................................................

.................................................................................

.................................................................................

# Evening

## HAPPINESS MANTRA

Today I felt gratitude for...

.................................................................................................

.................................................................................................

.................................................................................................

## EVENING MEDITATIONS

One thing I learned today was...

.................................................................................................

.................................................................................................

.................................................................................................

.................................................................................................

*I closed my eyes to focus on my breath, in and out, for a few minutes. These thoughts came to my mind...*

.................................................................................................

.................................................................................................

.................................................................................................

The most beautiful thing today was...

.................................................................................................

.................................................................................................

.................................................................................................

.................................................................................................

# Morning

Date ___ / ___ / ___

My intention today is...

.................................................................................................

.................................................................................................

.................................................................................................

.................................................................................................

## DIGITAL DETOX

I will turn off all my phones, tablets, and computers for..................................minutes.

My positive affirmation will be...

.................................................................................................

.................................................................................................

.................................................................................................

**I will take time to focus on...**

.........................................

.........................................

.........................................

.........................................

## NATURAL HEALING

I will harness nature's energy by...

.................................................................................................

.................................................................................................

.................................................................................................

.................................................................................................

# Evening

## HAPPINESS MANTRA

Today I felt gratitude for...

......................................................................................

......................................................................................

......................................................................................

## EVENING MEDITATIONS

One thing I learned today was...

...............................................................

...............................................................

...............................................................

*I closed my eyes to focus on my breath, in and out, for a few minutes. These thoughts came to my mind...*

............................................

............................................

............................................

The most beautiful thing today was...

......................................................................

......................................................................................

......................................................................................

......................................................................................

......................................................................................

# Morning

My intention today is...

.......................................................................................................

.......................................................................................................

.......................................................................................................

.......................................................................................................

## DIGITAL DETOX

I will turn off all my phones, tablets, and computers for.................................minutes.

My positive affirmation will be...

.......................................................................................................

.......................................................................................................

I will take time
to focus on...

..................................

..................................

..................................

..................................

## NATURAL HEALING

I will harness nature's energy by...

.......................................................................................................

.......................................................................................................

.......................................................................................................

# Evening

## HAPPINESS MANTRA

Today I felt gratitude for...

..................................................................................................................

..................................................................................................................

..................................................................................................................

## EVENING MEDITATIONS

One thing I learned today was...

..................................................................................................................

..................................................................................................................

..................................................................................................................

..................................................................................................................

*I closed my eyes to focus on my breath, in and out, for a few minutes. These thoughts came to my mind...*

..................................................

..................................................

..................................................

The most beautiful thing today was...

..................................................................................................................

..................................................................................................................

..................................................................................................................

..................................................................................................................

# Morning

My intention today is...

.............................................................................................................

.............................................................................................................

.............................................................................................................

.............................................................................................................

## DIGITAL DETOX

I will turn off all my phones, tablets, and computers for.............................................minutes.

My positive affirmation will be...

.............................................................................................................

.............................................................................................................

I will take time
to focus on...

...................................

...................................

...................................

...................................

## NATURAL HEALING

I will harness nature's energy by...

.............................................................................................................

.............................................................................................................

.............................................................................................................

.............................................................................................................

# Evening

## HAPPINESS MANTRA

Today I felt gratitude for...

.........................................................................................................

.........................................................................................................

.........................................................................................................

## EVENING MEDITATIONS

One thing I learned today was...

.........................................................................................................

.........................................................................................................

.........................................................................................................

.........................................................................................................

*I closed my eyes to focus on my breath, in and out, for a few minutes. These thoughts came to my mind...*

...........................................

...........................................

...........................................

The most beautiful thing today was...

.........................................................................................................

.........................................................................................................

.........................................................................................................

.........................................................................................................

 # Morning

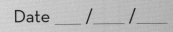

My intention today is...

.................................................................

.................................................................

.................................................................

.................................................................

.................................................................

.................................................................

## DIGITAL DETOX

I will turn off all my phones,

tablets, and computers

for.................................minutes.

I will take
time to focus on...

.................................................................

.................................................................

.................................................................

.................................................................

My positive affirmation will be...

.................................................................

.................................................................

.................................................................

.................................................................

.................................................................

.................................................................

## NATURAL HEALING

I will harness nature's energy by...

.................................................................

.................................................................

.................................................................

.................................................................

.................................................................

.................................................................

## HAPPINESS MANTRA

Today I felt gratitude for...

..................................................................................................................

..................................................................................................................

..................................................................................................................

## DAILY MINDFULNESS

One thing I learned today was...

..................................................................................................................

..................................................................................................................

..................................................................................................................

The most beautiful thing today was...

..................................................................................................................

..................................................................................................................

..................................................................................................................

*I closed my eyes to focus on my breath, in and out, for a few minutes. These thoughts came to my mind..................................................................................................................*

..................................................................................................................

 # Morning

Date ___ / ___ / ___

My intention today is...

..........................................................................

..........................................................................

..........................................................................

..........................................................................

..........................................................................

..........................................................................

### DIGITAL DETOX

I will turn off all my phones,

tablets, and computers

for...................................................minutes.

**I will take time to focus on...**

..........................................................

..........................................................

..........................................................

..........................................................

My positive affirmation will be...

..........................................................................

..........................................................................

..........................................................................

..........................................................................

..........................................................................

..........................................................................

### NATURAL HEALING

I will harness nature's energy by...

..........................................................................

..........................................................................

..........................................................................

..........................................................................

..........................................................................

..........................................................................

## HAPPINESS MANTRA

Today I felt gratitude for...

........................................................................................

........................................................................................

........................................................................................

## DAILY MINDFULNESS

One thing I learned today was...

........................................................................................

........................................................................................

The most beautiful thing today was...

........................................................................................

........................................................................................

........................................................................................

*I closed my eyes to focus on my breath, in and out, for a few minutes. These thoughts came to my mind.....................................................................*

........................................................................................

 # Morning

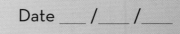 Date ___ / ___ / ___

My intention today is...

..........................................................................

..........................................................................

..........................................................................

..........................................................................

..........................................................................

..........................................................................

### DIGITAL DETOX

I will turn off all my phones,

tablets, and computers

for.........................................minutes.

I will take
time to focus on...

..........................................................................

..........................................................................

..........................................................................

..........................................................................

My positive affirmation will be...

..........................................................................

..........................................................................

..........................................................................

..........................................................................

..........................................................................

..........................................................................

### NATURAL HEALING

I will harness nature's energy by...

..........................................................................

..........................................................................

..........................................................................

..........................................................................

..........................................................................

..........................................................................

..........................................................................

# Evening 🌙

## HAPPINESS MANTRA

Today I felt gratitude for...

.......................................................................................................................

.......................................................................................................................

.......................................................................................................................

## DAILY MINDFULNESS

One thing I learned today was...

.......................................................................................................................

.......................................................................................................................

.......................................................................................................................

The most beautiful thing today was...

.......................................................................................................................

.......................................................................................................................

.......................................................................................................................

*I closed my eyes to focus on my breath, in and out, for a few minutes. These thoughts came to my mind.........................................................................................................*

.......................................................................................................................

 # Morning

Date ___ / ___ / ___

My intention today is...

..........................................................

..........................................................

..........................................................

..........................................................

..........................................................

..........................................................

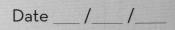

My positive affirmation will be...

..........................................................

..........................................................

..........................................................

..........................................................

..........................................................

### DIGITAL DETOX

I will turn off all my phones,

tablets, and computers

for...........................................minutes.

### NATURAL HEALING

I will harness nature's energy by...

..........................................................

..........................................................

..........................................................

..........................................................

I will take
time to focus on...

..........................................................

..........................................................

..........................................................

..........................................................

# Evening

## HAPPINESS MANTRA

Today I felt gratitude for...

..................................................................................................................

..................................................................................................................

..................................................................................................................

## DAILY MINDFULNESS

One thing I learned today was...

..................................................................................................................

..................................................................................................................

..................................................................................................................

The most beautiful thing today was...

..................................................................................................................

..................................................................................................................

..................................................................................................................

*I closed my eyes to focus on my breath, in and out, for a few minutes. These thoughts came to my mind....................................................................................................................*

*...............................................................................................................................*

 # Morning

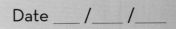 Date ___ / ___ / ___

My intention today is...

.........................................................

.........................................................

.........................................................

.........................................................

.........................................................

### DIGITAL DETOX

I will turn off all my phones,

tablets, and computers

for........................................minutes.

I will take
time to focus on...

.........................................................

.........................................................

.........................................................

.........................................................

My positive affirmation will be...

.........................................................

.........................................................

.........................................................

.........................................................

.........................................................

.........................................................

### NATURAL HEALING

I will harness nature's energy by...

.........................................................

.........................................................

.........................................................

.........................................................

.........................................................

## HAPPINESS MANTRA

Today I felt gratitude for...

.......................................................................................................

.......................................................................................................

.......................................................................................................

## DAILY MINDFULNESS

One thing I learned today was...

.......................................................................................................

.......................................................................................................

.......................................................................................................

The most beautiful thing today was...

.......................................................................................................

.......................................................................................................

.......................................................................................................

*I closed my eyes to focus on my breath, in and out, for a few minutes. These thoughts came to my mind*......................................................................................

.......................................................................................................

 # Morning

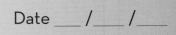

My intention today is...

........................................................
........................................................
........................................................
........................................................
........................................................
........................................................

## DIGITAL DETOX

I will turn off all my phones,

tablets, and computers

for................................................minutes.

### I will take
### time to focus on...

........................................................
........................................................
........................................................
........................................................

My positive affirmation will be...

........................................................
........................................................
........................................................
........................................................
........................................................

## NATURAL HEALING

I will harness nature's energy by...

........................................................
........................................................
........................................................
........................................................
........................................................
........................................................

## HAPPINESS MANTRA

Today I felt gratitude for...

......................................................................................................

......................................................................................................

......................................................................................................

## DAILY MINDFULNESS

One thing I learned today was...

......................................................................................................

......................................................................................................

......................................................................................................

The most beautiful thing today was...

......................................................................................................

......................................................................................................

......................................................................................................

*I closed my eyes to focus on my breath, in and out, for a few minutes. These thoughts came to my mind*......................................................................................

......................................................................................................

 **Morning**

Date ___ / ___ / ___

My intention today is...

..........................................................

..........................................................

..........................................................

..........................................................

..........................................................

..........................................................

### DIGITAL DETOX

I will turn off all my phones,

tablets, and computers

for.............................................minutes.

I will take
time to focus on...

..........................................................

..........................................................

..........................................................

..........................................................

My positive affirmation will be...

..........................................................

..........................................................

..........................................................

..........................................................

..........................................................

..........................................................

### NATURAL HEALING

I will harness nature's energy by...

..........................................................

..........................................................

..........................................................

..........................................................

..........................................................

## HAPPINESS MANTRA

Today I felt gratitude for...

........................................................................................................

........................................................................................................

........................................................................................................

## DAILY MINDFULNESS

One thing I learned today was...

........................................................................................................

........................................................................................................

........................................................................................................

The most beautiful thing today was...

........................................................................................................

........................................................................................................

........................................................................................................

*I closed my eyes to focus on my breath, in and out, for a few minutes. These thoughts came to my mind..........................................................................................*

........................................................................................................

 # Morning

My intention today is...

........................................................................

........................................................................

........................................................................

........................................................................

........................................................................

........................................................................

### DIGITAL DETOX

I will turn off all my phones,

tablets, and computers

for................................minutes.

I will take
time to focus on...

........................................................

........................................................

........................................................

........................................................

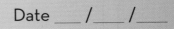

My positive affirmation will be...

........................................................................

........................................................................

........................................................................

........................................................................

........................................................................

........................................................................

### NATURAL HEALING

I will harness nature's energy by...

........................................................................

........................................................................

........................................................................

........................................................................

........................................................................

........................................................................

# Evening 🌙

## HAPPINESS MANTRA

Today I felt gratitude for...

......................................................................................................................

......................................................................................................................

......................................................................................................................

## DAILY MINDFULNESS

One thing I learned today was...

......................................................................................................................

......................................................................................................................

......................................................................................................................

The most beautiful thing today was...

......................................................................................................................

......................................................................................................................

......................................................................................................................

*I closed my eyes to focus on my breath, in and out, for a few minutes. These thoughts came to my mind*..............................................................................................................

......................................................................................................................

 # Morning

My intention today is...

........................................................

........................................................

........................................................

........................................................

........................................................

### DIGITAL DETOX

I will turn off all my phones,

tablets, and computers

for...............................minutes.

I will take
time to focus on...

........................................................

........................................................

........................................................

........................................................

My positive affirmation will be...

........................................................

........................................................

........................................................

........................................................

........................................................

........................................................

### NATURAL HEALING

I will harness nature's energy by...

........................................................

........................................................

........................................................

........................................................

........................................................

# Evening 🌙

## HAPPINESS MANTRA

Today I felt gratitude for...

......................................................................................

......................................................................................

......................................................................................

## DAILY MINDFULNESS

One thing I learned today was...

......................................................................................

......................................................................................

......................................................................................

The most beautiful thing today was...

......................................................................................

......................................................................................

......................................................................................

*I closed my eyes to focus on my breath, in and out, for a few minutes. These thoughts came to my mind*...................................................................................

......................................................................................

 # Morning

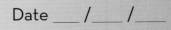 Date \_\_\_ / \_\_\_ / \_\_\_

My intention today is...

...........................................................

...........................................................

...........................................................

...........................................................

...........................................................

...........................................................

### DIGITAL DETOX

I will turn off all my phones,

tablets, and computers

for.................................minutes.

I will take
time to focus on...

...........................................................

...........................................................

...........................................................

...........................................................

My positive affirmation will be...

...........................................................

...........................................................

...........................................................

...........................................................

...........................................................

...........................................................

### NATURAL HEALING

I will harness nature's energy by...

...........................................................

...........................................................

...........................................................

...........................................................

...........................................................

...........................................................

## HAPPINESS MANTRA

Today I felt gratitude for...

..................................................................................................

..................................................................................................

..................................................................................................

## DAILY MINDFULNESS

One thing I learned today was...

..................................................................................................

..................................................................................................

..................................................................................................

The most beautiful thing today was...

..................................................................................................

..................................................................................................

..................................................................................................

*I closed my eyes to focus on my breath, in and out, for a few minutes. These thoughts came to my mind...........................................................................................*

..................................................................................................

 # Morning

My intention today is...

.........................................................

.........................................................

.........................................................

.........................................................

.........................................................

### DIGITAL DETOX

I will turn off all my phones,

tablets, and computers

for..........................................minutes.

I will take
time to focus on...

.........................................................

.........................................................

.........................................................

.........................................................

My positive affirmation will be...

.........................................................

.........................................................

.........................................................

.........................................................

.........................................................

.........................................................

### NATURAL HEALING

I will harness nature's energy by...

.........................................................

.........................................................

.........................................................

.........................................................

.........................................................

## HAPPINESS MANTRA

Today I felt gratitude for...

........................................................................

........................................................................

........................................................................

## DAILY MINDFULNESS

One thing I learned today was...

........................................................................

........................................................................

........................................................................

The most beautiful thing today was...

........................................................................

........................................................................

........................................................................

*I closed my eyes to focus on my breath, in and out, for a few minutes. These thoughts came to my mind.................................................................*

........................................................................

 # Morning

My intention today is...

..............................................................
..............................................................
..............................................................
..............................................................
..............................................................
..............................................................

## DIGITAL DETOX

I will turn off all my phones,

tablets, and computers

for.............................................minutes.

**I will take
time to focus on...**

..............................................
..............................................
..............................................
..............................................

My positive affirmation will be...

..............................................................
..............................................................
..............................................................
..............................................................
..............................................................

## NATURAL HEALING

I will harness nature's energy by...

..............................................................
..............................................................
..............................................................
..............................................................
..............................................................

## HAPPINESS MANTRA

Today I felt gratitude for...

..................................................................................................

..................................................................................................

..................................................................................................

## DAILY MINDFULNESS

One thing I learned today was...

..................................................................................................

..................................................................................................

..................................................................................................

The most beautiful thing today was...

..................................................................................................

..................................................................................................

..................................................................................................

*I closed my eyes to focus on my breath, in and out, for a few minutes. These thoughts came to my mind*..................................................................................................

..................................................................................................

 # Morning

My intention today is...

..................................................................

..................................................................

..................................................................

..................................................................

..................................................................

### DIGITAL DETOX

I will turn off all my phones,

tablets, and computers

for.................................................minutes.

### I will take
### time to focus on...

..................................................................

..................................................................

..................................................................

..................................................................

My positive affirmation will be...

..................................................................

..................................................................

..................................................................

..................................................................

..................................................................

..................................................................

### NATURAL HEALING

I will harness nature's energy by...

..................................................................

..................................................................

..................................................................

..................................................................

..................................................................

..................................................................

HAPPINESS MANTRA

Today I felt gratitude for...

.........................................................................................

.........................................................................................

.........................................................................................

DAILY MINDFULNESS

One thing I learned today was...

.........................................................................................

.........................................................................................

.........................................................................................

The most beautiful thing today was...

.........................................................................................

.........................................................................................

.........................................................................................

*I closed my eyes to focus on my breath, in and out, for a few minutes. These thoughts came to my mind*.........................................................................

.........................................................................................

# Morning

Date ___ / ___ / ___

My intention today is...

........................................................................................

........................................................................................

........................................................................................

## DIGITAL DETOX

I will turn off all my phones, tablets, and computers for........................................minutes.

My positive affirmation will be...

........................................................................................

........................................................................

........................................................................

I will take time to focus on...

........................................................................................

........................................................................................

........................................................................................

## NATURAL HEALING

I will harness nature's energy by...

........................................................................................

........................................................................................

........................................................................................

........................................................................................

# Evening

## HAPPINESS MANTRA

Today I felt gratitude for...

.................................................................................................

.................................................................................................

.................................................................................................

.................................................................................................

*I closed my eyes for a few minutes to focus on my breath, in and out. These thoughts arose in my mind...*

.................................................................

.................................................................

.................................................................

.................................................................

## EVENING MEDITATIONS

One thing I learned today was...

.................................................................................................

.................................................................................................

.................................................................................................

.................................................................................................

The most beautiful thing today was...

.................................................................................................

.................................................................................................

.................................................................................................

# Morning

Date ___ / ___ / ___

My intention today is...

..............................................................................................................

..............................................................................................................

..............................................................................................................

## DIGITAL DETOX

I will turn off all my phones, tablets, and computers for.................................minutes.

My positive affirmation will be...

..............................................................................................................

..............................................................................................................

..............................................................................................................

I will take time to focus on...

..............................................................................................................

..............................................................................................................

..............................................................................................................

## NATURAL HEALING

I will harness nature's energy by...

..............................................................................................................

..............................................................................................................

..............................................................................................................

..............................................................................................................

# Evening

## HAPPINESS MANTRA

Today I felt gratitude for...

...........................................................................................................

...........................................................................................................

...........................................................................................................

...........................................................................................................

*I closed my eyes for a few minutes to focus on my breath, in and out. These thoughts arose in my mind...*

...................................................

...................................................

...................................................

.......................

## EVENING MEDITATIONS

One thing I learned today was...

...........................................................................................................

...........................................................................................................

...........................................................................................................

...........................................................................................................

The most beautiful thing today was...

...........................................................................................................

...........................................................................................................

...........................................................................................................

# Morning

Date ___ / ___ / ___

My intention today is...

..................................................................................................

..................................................................................................

..................................................................................................

## DIGITAL DETOX

I will turn off all my phones, tablets, and computers for.................................................minutes.

My positive affirmation will be...

..................................................................................................

..................................................................................................

..................................................................................................

I will take time to focus on...

..................................................................................................

..................................................................................................

..................................................................................................

## NATURAL HEALING

I will harness nature's energy by...

..................................................................................................

..................................................................................................

..................................................................................................

..................................................................................................

# Evening

## HAPPINESS MANTRA

Today I felt gratitude for...

.................................................................................................

.................................................................................................

.................................................................................................

.................................................................................................

*I closed my eyes for a few minutes to focus on my breath, in and out. These thoughts arose in my mind...*

.................................................................

.................................................................

.................................................................

.........................

## EVENING MEDITATIONS

One thing I learned today was...

.................................................................................................

.................................................................................................

.................................................................................................

.................................................................................................

The most beautiful thing today was...

.................................................................................................

.................................................................................................

.................................................................................................

# Morning

Date ___ / ___ / ___

My intention today is...

.......................................................................................................................

.......................................................................................................................

.......................................................................................................................

## DIGITAL DETOX

I will turn off all my phones, tablets, and computers for...................................minutes.

My positive affirmation will be...

.......................................................................................................................

.......................................................................................................

.......................................................................

I will take time to focus on...

.......................................................................

.......................................................................

.......................................................................

## NATURAL HEALING

I will harness nature's energy by...

.......................................................................................................................

.......................................................................................................................

.......................................................................................................................

.......................................................................................................................

# Evening

## HAPPINESS MANTRA

Today I felt gratitude for...

..............................................................................................

..............................................................................................

..............................................................................................

..............................................................................................

*I closed my eyes for a few minutes to focus on my breath, in and out. These thoughts arose in my mind...*

..........................................................

..........................................................

..........................................................

....................

## EVENING MEDITATIONS

One thing I learned today was...

..............................................................................................

..............................................................................................

..............................................................................................

The most beautiful thing today was...

..............................................................................................

..............................................................................................

# Morning

My intention today is...

.................................................................................................................

.................................................................................................................

.................................................................................................................

## DIGITAL DETOX

I will turn off all my phones, tablets, and computers for........................................minutes.

My positive affirmation will be...

.................................................................................................................

.................................................................................................................

.................................................................................................................

I will take time to focus on...

.................................................................................................................

.................................................................................................................

.................................................................................................................

## NATURAL HEALING

I will harness nature's energy by...

.................................................................................................................

.................................................................................................................

.................................................................................................................

.................................................................................................................

# Evening

## HAPPINESS MANTRA

Today I felt gratitude for...

..............................................................................................

..............................................................................................

..............................................................................................

..............................................................................................

*I closed my eyes for a few minutes to focus on my breath, in and out. These thoughts arose in my mind...*

..............................................................

..............................................................

..............................................................

..............................

## EVENING MEDITATIONS

One thing I learned today was...

..............................................................................................

..............................................................................................

..............................................................................................

..............................................................................................

The most beautiful thing today was...

..............................................................................................

..............................................................................................

..............................................................................................

# Morning

Date ___ / ___ / ___

My intention today is...

.................................................................................................

.................................................................................................

.................................................................................................

## DIGITAL DETOX

I will turn off all my phones, tablets, and computers for.............................minutes.

My positive affirmation will be...

.................................................................................................

.................................................................................................

.................................................................................................

I will take time to focus on...

.................................................................................................

.................................................................................................

.................................................................................................

## NATURAL HEALING

I will harness nature's energy by...

.................................................................................................

.................................................................................................

.................................................................................................

.................................................................................................

# Evening

## HAPPINESS MANTRA

Today I felt gratitude for...

..............................................................................................

..............................................................................................

..............................................................................................

..............................................................................................

*I closed my eyes for a few minutes to focus on my breath, in and out. These thoughts arose in my mind...*

......................................................

......................................................

......................................................

......................................

## EVENING MEDITATIONS

One thing I learned today was...

..............................................................................................

..............................................................................................

..............................................................................................

The most beautiful thing today was...

..............................................................................................

..............................................................................................

..............................................................................................

# Morning

Date ___ / ___ / ___

My intention today is...

........................................................................................................................

........................................................................................................................

........................................................................................................................

## DIGITAL DETOX

I will turn off all my phones, tablets, and computers for...........................minutes.

My positive affirmation will be...

........................................................................................................................

.................................................................................................

.................................................................................

I will take time to focus on...

........................................................................

........................................................................

........................................................................

## NATURAL HEALING

I will harness nature's energy by...

........................................................................................................................

........................................................................................................................

........................................................................................................................

........................................................................................................................

# Evening

## HAPPINESS MANTRA

Today I felt gratitude for...

...........................................................................................

...........................................................................................

...........................................................................................

*I closed my eyes
for a few minutes to focus
on my breath, in and out. These
thoughts arose in my mind...*

...................................................

...................................................

...................................................

...................................

## EVENING MEDITATIONS

One thing I learned today was...

...........................................................................................

...........................................................................................

...........................................................................................

The most beautiful thing today was...

...........................................................................................

...........................................................................................

...........................................................................................

# Morning

My intention today is...

....................................................................................................

....................................................................................................

....................................................................................................

## DIGITAL DETOX

I will turn off all my phones, tablets, and computers for...........................................minutes.

My positive affirmation will be...

....................................................................................................

....................................................................................................

I will take time to focus on...

....................................................................................................

....................................................................................................

....................................................................................................

## NATURAL HEALING

I will harness nature's energy by...

....................................................................................................

....................................................................................................

....................................................................................................

# Evening

## HAPPINESS MANTRA

Today I felt gratitude for...

......................................................................................................

......................................................................................................

......................................................................................................

......................................................................................................

*I closed my eyes for a few minutes to focus on my breath, in and out. These thoughts arose in my mind...*

......................................................................

......................................................................

......................................................................

.........................................

## EVENING MEDITATIONS

One thing I learned today was...

......................................................................................................

......................................................................................................

......................................................................................................

......................................................................................................

The most beautiful thing today was...

......................................................................................................

......................................................................................................

......................................................................................................

# Morning

Date ___ / ___ / ___

### My intention today is...

...................................................................................................

...................................................................................................

...................................................................................................

## DIGITAL DETOX

I will turn off all my phones, tablets, and computers for..............................minutes.

My positive affirmation will be...

...................................................................................................

...................................................................................

...............................................................

I will take time to focus on...

......................................................

......................................................

......................................................

## NATURAL HEALING

I will harness nature's energy by...

...................................................................................................

...................................................................................................

...................................................................................................

...................................................................................................

# Evening

## HAPPINESS MANTRA

Today I felt gratitude for...

.............................................................................

.............................................................................

.............................................................................

.............................................................................

*I closed my eyes for a few minutes to focus on my breath, in and out. These thoughts arose in my mind...*

.............................................................

.............................................................

.............................................................

.................................

## EVENING MEDITATIONS

One thing I learned today was...

.............................................................................

.............................................................................

.............................................................................

.............................................................................

The most beautiful thing today was...

.............................................................................

.............................................................................

.............................................................................

# Morning

Date ___ / ___ / ___

## My intention today is...

........................................................................................

........................................................................................

........................................................................................

## DIGITAL DETOX

I will turn off all my phones, tablets, and computers for.................................................minutes.

My positive affirmation will be...

........................................................................................

........................................................................................

........................................................................................

### I will take time to focus on...

........................................................................................

........................................................................................

........................................................................................

## NATURAL HEALING

I will harness nature's energy by...

........................................................................................

........................................................................................

........................................................................................

........................................................................................

# Evening

## HAPPINESS MANTRA

Today I felt gratitude for...

..............................................................................

..............................................................................

..............................................................................

..............................................................................

*I closed my eyes for a few minutes to focus on my breath, in and out. These thoughts arose in my mind...*

..............................................................

..............................................................

..............................................................

..............................

## EVENING MEDITATIONS

One thing I learned today was...

..............................................................................

..............................................................................

..............................................................................

The most beautiful thing today was...

..............................................................................

..............................................................................

..............................................................................

# Morning

Date ___ / ___ / ___

## My intention today is...

........................................................................................................................

........................................................................................................................

........................................................................................................................

## DIGITAL DETOX

I will turn off all my phones, tablets, and computers for.............................................minutes.

My positive affirmation will be...

........................................................................................................................

........................................................................................................

........................................................................................

I will take time to focus on...

........................................................................................

........................................................................................

........................................................................................

## NATURAL HEALING

I will harness nature's energy by...

........................................................................................................................

........................................................................................................................

........................................................................................................................

........................................................................................................................

# Evening

## HAPPINESS MANTRA

Today I felt gratitude for...

......................................................................................

......................................................................................

......................................................................................

......................................................................................

*I closed my eyes for a few minutes to focus on my breath, in and out. These thoughts arose in my mind...*

..............................................

..............................................

..............................................

..................

## EVENING MEDITATIONS

One thing I learned today was...

......................................................................................

......................................................................................

......................................................................................

......................................................................................

The most beautiful thing today was...

......................................................................................

......................................................................................

......................................................................................

# Morning

Date ___ / ___ / ___

My intention today is...

.......................................................................................................................

.......................................................................................................................

.......................................................................................................................

## DIGITAL DETOX

I will turn off all my phones, tablets, and computers for...................................minutes.

My positive affirmation will be...

.......................................................................................................................

...............................................................................................

.................................................................................

I will take time to focus on...

.......................................................................

.......................................................................

.......................................................................

## NATURAL HEALING

I will harness nature's energy by...

.......................................................................................................................

.......................................................................................................................

.......................................................................................................................

.......................................................................................................................

# Evening

## HAPPINESS MANTRA

Today I felt gratitude for...

......................................................................................

......................................................................................

......................................................................................

......................................................................................

*I closed my eyes for a few minutes to focus on my breath, in and out. These thoughts arose in my mind...*

......................................................

......................................................

......................................................

......................................................

## EVENING MEDITATIONS

One thing I learned today was...

......................................................................................

......................................................................................

......................................................................................

The most beautiful thing today was...

......................................................................................

......................................................................................

......................................................................................

# Morning

Date ___ / ___ / ___

My intention today is...

........................................................................................

........................................................................................

........................................................................................

## DIGITAL DETOX

I will turn off all my phones, tablets, and computers for.........................minutes.

My positive affirmation will be...

........................................................................................

........................................................................

................................................................

I will take time to focus on...

........................................................

........................................................

........................................................

## NATURAL HEALING

I will harness nature's energy by...

........................................................................................

........................................................................................

........................................................................................

........................................................................................

# Evening

## HAPPINESS MANTRA

Today I felt gratitude for...

.............................................................................

.............................................................................

.............................................................................

.............................................................................

*I closed my eyes for a few minutes to focus on my breath, in and out. These thoughts arose in my mind...*

.............................................................

.............................................................

.............................................................

.............................

## EVENING MEDITATIONS

One thing I learned today was...

.............................................................................

.............................................................................

.............................................................................

.............................................................................

The most beautiful thing today was...

.............................................................................

.............................................................................

.............................................................................

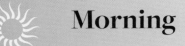

# Morning

Date ___ / ___ / ___

My intention today is...

..............................................................................................

..............................................................................................

..............................................................................................

## DIGITAL DETOX

I will turn off all my phones, tablets, and computers for........................minutes.

My positive affirmation will be ...

..............................................................................................

..............................................................................................

## NATURAL HEALING

I will harness nature's energy by...

..............................................................................................

..............................................................................................

..............................................................................................

I will take time to focus on...

..............................................................................................

..............................................................................................

..............................................................................................

# Evening

### HAPPINESS MANTRA

Today I felt gratitude for...

......................................................................

......................................................................

......................................................................

### DAILY MINDFULNESS

One thing I learned today was...

......................................................................

......................................................................

The most beautiful thing today was...

......................................................................

......................................................................

......................................................................

*I closed my eyes for a few minutes to focus on my breath, in and out. These thoughts arose in my mind...*

......................................................................

......................................................................

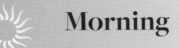

# Morning

Date ___ / ___ / ___

My intention today is...

..............................................................................................................

..............................................................................................................

..............................................................................................................

### DIGITAL DETOX

I will turn off all my phones, tablets, and computers for.............................minutes.

My positive affirmation will be ...

..............................................................................................................

..............................................................................................................

### NATURAL HEALING

I will harness nature's energy by...

..............................................................................................................

..............................................................................................................

..............................................................................................................

I will take time to focus on...

..............................................................................................

..............................................................................................

..............................................................................................

## HAPPINESS MANTRA

Today I felt gratitude for...

..................................................................................

..................................................................................

..................................................................................

## DAILY MINDFULNESS

One thing I learned today was...

..................................................................................

..................................................................................

The most beautiful thing today was...

..................................................................................

..................................................................................

..................................................................................

*I closed my eyes for a few minutes to focus on my breath, in and out. These thoughts arose in my mind...*

..................................................................................

..................................................................................

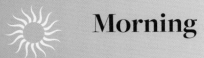 # Morning

My intention today is...

.............................................................................................................................

.............................................................................................................................

.............................................................................................................................

## DIGITAL DETOX

I will turn off all my phones, tablets, and computers for........................minutes.

My positive affirmation will be ...

.............................................................................................................................

.............................................................................................................................

## NATURAL HEALING

I will harness nature's energy by...

.............................................................................................................................

.............................................................................................................................

.............................................................................................................................

I will take time to focus on...

.....................................................................

.....................................................................

.....................................................................

# Evening

### HAPPINESS MANTRA

Today I felt gratitude for...

..................................................................................................................

..................................................................................................................

..................................................................................................................

### DAILY MINDFULNESS

One thing I learned today was...

..................................................................................................................

..................................................................................................................

The most beautiful thing today was...

..................................................................................................................

..................................................................................................................

..................................................................................................................

*I closed my eyes for a few minutes to focus on my breath, in and out. These thoughts arose in my mind...*

..................................................................................................

..................................................................................................

# Morning

Date ___ / ___ / ___

My intention today is...

........................................................................................................

........................................................................................................

........................................................................................................

## DIGITAL DETOX

I will turn off all my phones, tablets, and computers for.............................minutes.

My positive affirmation will be ...

........................................................................................................

........................................................................................................

## NATURAL HEALING

I will harness nature's energy by...

........................................................................................................

........................................................................................................

........................................................................................................

I will take time to focus on...

..................................................................

..................................................................

..................................................................

# Evening

## HAPPINESS MANTRA

Today I felt gratitude for...

......................................................................................

......................................................................................

......................................................................................

## DAILY MINDFULNESS

One thing I learned today was...

......................................................................................

......................................................................................

The most beautiful thing today was...

......................................................................................

......................................................................................

......................................................................................

*I closed my eyes for a few minutes to focus on my breath, in and out. These thoughts arose in my mind...*

......................................................................................

......................................................................................

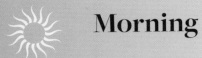

# Morning

My intention today is...

........................................................................................................

........................................................................................................

........................................................................................................

## DIGITAL DETOX

I will turn off all my phones, tablets, and computers for............................minutes.

My positive affirmation will be ...

........................................................................................................

........................................................................................................

## NATURAL HEALING

I will harness nature's energy by...

........................................................................................................

........................................................................................................

........................................................................................................

I will take time to focus on...

........................................................................................

........................................................................................

........................................................................................

# Evening

### HAPPINESS MANTRA

Today I felt gratitude for...

.........................................................................................................

.........................................................................................................

.........................................................................................................

### DAILY MINDFULNESS

One thing I learned today was...

.........................................................................................................

.........................................................................................................

The most beautiful thing today was...

.........................................................................................................

.........................................................................................................

.........................................................................................................

*I closed my eyes for a few minutes to focus on my breath, in and out. These thoughts arose in my mind...*

.........................................................................................

.........................................................................................

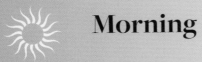

# Morning

Date ___ / ___ / ___

## My intention today is...

...............................................................................................................

...............................................................................................................

...............................................................................................................

### DIGITAL DETOX

I will turn off all my phones, tablets, and computers for.............................minutes.

### My positive affirmation will be ...

...............................................................................................................

...............................................................................................................

### NATURAL HEALING

I will harness nature's energy by...

...............................................................................................................

...............................................................................................................

...............................................................................................................

### I will take time to focus on...

........................................................................................

........................................................................................

........................................................................................

# Evening

### HAPPINESS MANTRA

Today I felt gratitude for...

.................................................................................................

.................................................................................................

.................................................................................................

### DAILY MINDFULNESS

One thing I learned today was...

.................................................................................................

.................................................................................................

The most beautiful thing today was...

.................................................................................................

.................................................................................................

.................................................................................................

*I closed my eyes for a few minutes to focus on my breath, in and out. These thoughts arose in my mind...*

.................................................................................................

.................................................................................................

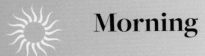

# Morning

Date ___ / ___ / ___

My intention today is...

.............................................................................................................

.............................................................................................................

.............................................................................................................

## DIGITAL DETOX

I will turn off all my phones, tablets, and computers for...........................minutes.

My positive affirmation will be ...

.............................................................................................................

.............................................................................................................

## NATURAL HEALING

I will harness nature's energy by...

.............................................................................................................

.............................................................................................................

.............................................................................................................

I will take time to focus on...

.................................................................................

.................................................................................

.................................................................................

# Evening

## HAPPINESS MANTRA

Today I felt gratitude for...

..................................................................

..................................................................

..................................................................

## DAILY MINDFULNESS

One thing I learned today was...

..................................................................

..................................................................

The most beautiful thing today was...

..................................................................

..................................................................

..................................................................

*I closed my eyes for a few minutes to focus on my breath, in and out. These thoughts arose in my mind...*

..................................................................

..................................................................

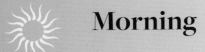

# Morning

Date ___ / ___ / ___

My intention today is...

.................................................................................................

.................................................................................................

.................................................................................................

## DIGITAL DETOX

I will turn off all my phones, tablets, and computers for.............................minutes.

My positive affirmation will be ...

.................................................................................................

.................................................................................................

## NATURAL HEALING

I will harness nature's energy by...

.................................................................................................

.................................................................................................

.................................................................................................

I will take time to focus on...

.................................................................................................

.................................................................................................

.................................................................................................

# Evening

## HAPPINESS MANTRA

### Today I felt gratitude for...

..................................................................................................

..................................................................................................

..................................................................................................

## DAILY MINDFULNESS

### One thing I learned today was...

..................................................................................................

..................................................................................................

### The most beautiful thing today was...

..................................................................................................

..................................................................................................

..................................................................................................

*I closed my eyes for a few minutes to focus on my breath, in and out. These thoughts arose in my mind...*

..................................................................................................

..................................................................................................

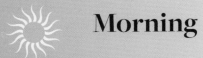

# Morning

My intention today is...

.......................................................................................................................

.......................................................................................................................

.......................................................................................................................

## DIGITAL DETOX

I will turn off all my phones, tablets, and computers for...........................minutes.

My positive affirmation will be ...

.......................................................................................................................

.......................................................................................................................

## NATURAL HEALING

I will harness nature's energy by...

.......................................................................................................................

.......................................................................................................................

.......................................................................................................................

I will take time to focus on...

.................................................................................

.................................................................................

.................................................................................

# Evening

## HAPPINESS MANTRA

Today I felt gratitude for...

..................................................................

..................................................................

..................................................................

## DAILY MINDFULNESS

One thing I learned today was...

..................................................................

..................................................................

The most beautiful thing today was...

..................................................................

..................................................................

..................................................................

*I closed my eyes for a few minutes to focus on my breath, in and out. These thoughts arose in my mind...*

..................................................................

..................................................................

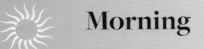

# Morning

My intention today is...

......................................................................................................................

......................................................................................................................

......................................................................................................................

### DIGITAL DETOX

I will turn off all my phones, tablets, and computers for........................minutes.

My positive affirmation will be ...

......................................................................................................................

......................................................................................................................

### NATURAL HEALING

I will harness nature's energy by...

......................................................................................................................

......................................................................................................................

......................................................................................................................

I will take time to focus on...

......................................................................................................

......................................................................................................

......................................................................................................

# Evening

### HAPPINESS MANTRA

Today I felt gratitude for...

.......................................................................................................

.......................................................................................................

.......................................................................................................

### DAILY MINDFULNESS

One thing I learned today was...

.......................................................................................................

.......................................................................................................

The most beautiful thing today was...

.......................................................................................................

.......................................................................................................

.......................................................................................................

*I closed my eyes for a few minutes to focus on my breath, in and out. These thoughts arose in my mind...*

.......................................................................................

.......................................................................................

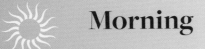

# Morning

My intention today is...

..............................................................................................................

..............................................................................................................

..............................................................................................................

## DIGITAL DETOX

I will turn off all my phones, tablets, and computers for.............................minutes.

My positive affirmation will be ...

..............................................................................................................

..............................................................................................................

## NATURAL HEALING

I will harness nature's energy by...

..............................................................................................................

..............................................................................................................

..............................................................................................................

I will take time to focus on...

..............................................................................................................

..............................................................................................................

..............................................................................................................

# Evening

### HAPPINESS MANTRA

Today I felt gratitude for...

............................................................................................

............................................................................................

............................................................................................

### DAILY MINDFULNESS

One thing I learned today was...

............................................................................................

............................................................................................

The most beautiful thing today was...

............................................................................................

............................................................................................

............................................................................................

*I closed my eyes for a few minutes to focus on my breath, in and out. These thoughts arose in my mind...*

............................................................................................

............................................................................................

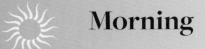

# Morning

Date ___ / ___ / ___

My intention today is...

.............................................................................................................
.............................................................................................................
.............................................................................................................

## DIGITAL DETOX

I will turn off all my phones, tablets, and computers for........................minutes.

My positive affirmation will be ...

.............................................................................................................
.............................................................................................................

## NATURAL HEALING

I will harness nature's energy by...

.............................................................................................................
.............................................................................................................
.............................................................................................................

I will take time to focus on...

.............................................................................................................
.............................................................................................................

# Evening

HAPPINESS MANTRA

Today I felt gratitude for...

.......................................................................................

.......................................................................................

.......................................................................................

DAILY MINDFULNESS

One thing I learned today was...

.......................................................................................

.......................................................................................

.......................................................................................

The most beautiful thing today was...

.......................................................................................

.......................................................................................

.......................................................................................

*I closed my eyes for a few minutes to focus on my breath, in and out. These thoughts arose in my mind...*

.......................................................................................

.......................................................................................

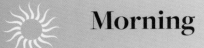 # Morning

My intention today is...

.......................................................................................................................

.......................................................................................................................

.......................................................................................................................

## DIGITAL DETOX

I will turn off all my phones, tablets, and computers for.............................minutes.

My positive affirmation will be ...

.......................................................................................................................

.......................................................................................................................

## NATURAL HEALING

I will harness nature's energy by...

.......................................................................................................................

.......................................................................................................................

.......................................................................................................................

I will take time to focus on...

.......................................................................................................................

.......................................................................................................................

.......................................................................................................................

# Evening

### HAPPINESS MANTRA

Today I felt gratitude for...

.................................................................................

.................................................................................

.................................................................................

### DAILY MINDFULNESS

One thing I learned today was...

.................................................................................

.................................................................................

The most beautiful thing today was...

.................................................................................

.................................................................................

.................................................................................

*I closed my eyes for a few minutes to focus on my breath, in and out. These thoughts arose in my mind...*

.................................................................................

.................................................................................

# Morning

Date ___ / ___ / ___

My intention today is...

.................................................................................

.................................................................................

.................................................................................

.................................................................................

I will take
time to focus on...

.................................................................................

.................................................................................

.................................................................................

.................................................................................

## DIGITAL DETOX

I will turn off all my phones, tablets, and

computers for.............................................minutes.

My positive affirmation will be...

.................................................................................

.................................................................................

.................................................................................

## NATURAL HEALING

I will harness nature's energy by...

.................................................................................

.................................................................................

.................................................................................

# Evening

*I closed my eyes for a few minutes to focus on my breath, in and out. These thoughts arose in my mind...*

................................................

................................................

................................................

## HAPPINESS MANTRA

Today I felt gratitude for...

................................................

................................................

................................................

................................................

................................................

## EVENING MEDITATIONS

One thing I learned today was...

................................................

................................................

................................................

................................................

The most beautiful thing today was...

................................................

................................................

................................................

................................................

# Morning

Date ___ / ___ / ___

My intention today is...

....................................................................................

....................................................................................

....................................................................................

....................................................................................

I will take
time to focus on...

....................................................................

....................................................................

....................................................................

## DIGITAL DETOX

I will turn off all my phones, tablets, and

computers for.................................................minutes.

My positive affirmation will be...

....................................................................................

....................................................................................

....................................................................................

## NATURAL HEALING

I will harness nature's energy by...

....................................................................................

....................................................................................

....................................................................................

# Evening

*I closed my eyes for a few minutes to focus on my breath, in and out. These thoughts arose in my mind...*

.........................................................

.........................................................

.........................................................

.........................................................

## HAPPINESS MANTRA

Today I felt gratitude for...

.........................................................

.........................................................

.........................................................

.........................................................

## EVENING MEDITATIONS

One thing I learned today was...

.........................................................

.........................................................

.........................................................

.........................................................

The most beautiful thing today was...

.........................................................

.........................................................

.........................................................

# Morning

Date ___ / ___ / ___

My intention today is...

........................................................................

........................................................................

........................................................................

........................................................................

I will take
time to focus on...

........................................

........................................

........................................

## DIGITAL DETOX

I will turn off all my phones, tablets, and

computers for.............................................minutes.

My positive affirmation will be...

........................................................................

........................................................................

........................................................................

## NATURAL HEALING

I will harness nature's energy by...

........................................................................

........................................................................

........................................................................

# Evening

*I closed my eyes for a few minutes to focus on my breath, in and out. These thoughts arose in my mind...*

...........................................

...........................................

...........................................

## HAPPINESS MANTRA

Today I felt gratitude for...

...........................................

...........................................

...........................................

...........................................

## EVENING MEDITATIONS

One thing I learned today was...

...........................................

...........................................

...........................................

...........................................

The most beautiful thing today was...

...........................................

...........................................

...........................................

# Morning

Date ___ / ___ / ___

My intention today is...

........................................................................

........................................................................

........................................................................

........................................................................

I will take
time to focus on...

........................................................................

........................................................................

........................................................................

## DIGITAL DETOX

I will turn off all my phones, tablets, and

computers for.........................................minutes.

My positive affirmation will be...

........................................................................

........................................................................

........................................................................

## NATURAL HEALING

I will harness nature's energy by...

........................................................................

........................................................................

........................................................................

# Evening

*I closed my eyes for a few minutes to focus on my breath, in and out. These thoughts arose in my mind...*

........................................

........................................

........................................

## HAPPINESS MANTRA

Today I felt gratitude for...

...................................................................

...................................................................

...................................................................

...................................................................

...................................................................

## EVENING MEDITATIONS

One thing I learned today was...

...................................................................

...................................................................

...................................................................

...................................................................

The most beautiful thing today was...

...................................................................

...................................................................

...................................................................

# **Morning**

Date ___ / ___ / ___

My intention today is...

.............................................................................

.............................................................................

.............................................................................

.............................................................................

I will take
time to focus on...

.............................................................

.............................................................

## DIGITAL DETOX

I will turn off all my phones, tablets, and

computers for...................................................minutes.

My positive affirmation will be...

.................................................................................

.................................................................................

.................................................................................

## NATURAL HEALING

I will harness nature's energy by...

.................................................................................

.................................................................................

.................................................................................

# Evening

*I closed my eyes for a few minutes to focus on my breath, in and out. These thoughts arose in my mind...*

.................................

.................................

.................................

## HAPPINESS MANTRA

Today I felt gratitude for...

.................................

.................................

.................................

.................................

## EVENING MEDITATIONS

One thing I learned today was...

.................................

.................................

.................................

.................................

The most beautiful thing today was...

.................................

.................................

.................................

# Morning

Date ___ / ___ / ___

My intention today is...

..................................................................

..................................................................

..................................................................

..................................................................

I will take
time to focus on...

.......................................

.......................................

.......................................

## DIGITAL DETOX

I will turn off all my phones, tablets, and

computers for...............................minutes.

My positive affirmation will be...

..................................................................

..................................................................

..................................................................

## NATURAL HEALING

I will harness nature's energy by...

..................................................................

..................................................................

..................................................................

# Evening

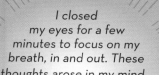

*I closed my eyes for a few minutes to focus on my breath, in and out. These thoughts arose in my mind...*

...............................................

...............................................

...............................................

## HAPPINESS MANTRA

Today I felt gratitude for...

...............................................................

...............................................................

...............................................................

...............................................................

## EVENING MEDITATIONS

One thing I learned today was...

...............................................................................................

...............................................................................................

...............................................................................................

...............................................................................................

The most beautiful thing today was...

...............................................................................................

...............................................................................................

...............................................................................................

# Morning

Date ___ / ___ / ___

My intention today is...

....................................................................

....................................................................

....................................................................

....................................................................

I will take
time to focus on...

....................................................

....................................................

## DIGITAL DETOX

I will turn off all my phones, tablets, and

computers for.....................................minutes.

My positive affirmation will be...

....................................................................

....................................................................

....................................................................

## NATURAL HEALING

I will harness nature's energy by...

....................................................................

....................................................................

....................................................................

# Evening

*I closed my eyes for a few minutes to focus on my breath, in and out. These thoughts arose in my mind...*

........................................

........................................

........................................

## HAPPINESS MANTRA

Today I felt gratitude for...

....................................................

....................................................

....................................................

....................................................

....................................................

## EVENING MEDITATIONS

One thing I learned today was...

....................................................................

....................................................................

....................................................................

....................................................................

The most beautiful thing today was...

....................................................................

....................................................................

....................................................................

# Morning

My intention today is...

..............................................................................

..............................................................................

..............................................................................

..............................................................................

I will take
time to focus on...

..............................................

..............................................

..............................................

..............................................

## DIGITAL DETOX

I will turn off all my phones, tablets, and

computers for.............................................minutes.

My positive affirmation will be...

..............................................................................

..............................................................................

..............................................................................

## NATURAL HEALING

I will harness nature's energy by...

..............................................................................

..............................................................................

..............................................................................

# Evening

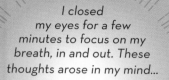

*I closed my eyes for a few minutes to focus on my breath, in and out. These thoughts arose in my mind...*

.............................................

.............................................

.............................................

.............................................

## HAPPINESS MANTRA

Today I felt gratitude for...

.............................................

.............................................

.............................................

.............................................

## EVENING MEDITATIONS

One thing I learned today was...

.............................................

.............................................

.............................................

.............................................

The most beautiful thing today was...

.............................................

.............................................

.............................................

# Morning

Date ___ / ___ / ___

My intention today is...

.................................................................................

.................................................................................

.................................................................................

.................................................................................

I will take
time to focus on...

.................................................

.................................................

.................................................

## DIGITAL DETOX

I will turn off all my phones, tablets, and

computers for.................................................minutes.

My positive affirmation will be...

.................................................................................

.................................................................................

.................................................................................

## NATURAL HEALING

I will harness nature's energy by...

.................................................................................

.................................................................................

.................................................................................

# Evening

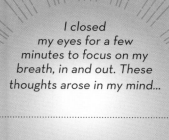

*I closed my eyes for a few minutes to focus on my breath, in and out. These thoughts arose in my mind...*

......................................................

......................................................

......................................................

## HAPPINESS MANTRA

Today I felt gratitude for...

......................................................

......................................................

......................................................

......................................................

......................................................

## EVENING MEDITATIONS

One thing I learned today was...

......................................................

......................................................

......................................................

......................................................

The most beautiful thing today was...

......................................................

......................................................

......................................................

# Morning

Date ___ / ___ / ___

My intention today is...

........................................................................
........................................................................
........................................................................
........................................................................

I will take
time to focus on...

........................................................
........................................................
........................................................

## DIGITAL DETOX

I will turn off all my phones, tablets, and

computers for.................................................minutes.

My positive affirmation will be...

........................................................................
........................................................................
........................................................................

## NATURAL HEALING

I will harness nature's energy by...

........................................................................
........................................................................
........................................................................

# Evening

*I closed my eyes for a few minutes to focus on my breath, in and out. These thoughts arose in my mind...*

.........................................

.........................................

.........................................

## HAPPINESS MANTRA

Today I felt gratitude for...

.................................................................

.................................................................

.................................................................

.................................................................

.................................................................

## EVENING MEDITATIONS

One thing I learned today was...

.................................................................

.................................................................

.................................................................

.................................................................

The most beautiful thing today was...

.................................................................

.................................................................

.................................................................

# Morning

Date ___ / ___ / ___

My intention today is...

............................................................................................

............................................................................................

............................................................................................

............................................................................................

**I will take time to focus on...**

............................................................

............................................................

............................................................

............................................................

## DIGITAL DETOX

I will turn off all my phones, tablets, and computers for.........................................minutes.

My positive affirmation will be...

............................................................................................

............................................................................................

............................................................................................

## NATURAL HEALING

I will harness nature's energy by...

............................................................................................

............................................................................................

............................................................................................

# Evening

*I closed my eyes for a few minutes to focus on my breath, in and out. These thoughts arose in my mind...*

........................................

........................................

........................................

## HAPPINESS MANTRA

Today I felt gratitude for...

........................................

........................................

........................................

........................................

........................................

## EVENING MEDITATIONS

One thing I learned today was...

........................................

........................................

........................................

........................................

The most beautiful thing today was...

........................................

........................................

........................................

# **Morning**

Date ___ / ___ / ___

My intention today is...

....................................................................

....................................................................

....................................................................

....................................................................

I will take
time to focus on...

....................................................

....................................................

....................................................

....................................................

DIGITAL DETOX

I will turn off all my phones, tablets, and

computers for.................................................minutes.

My positive affirmation will be...

....................................................................................

....................................................................................

....................................................................................

NATURAL HEALING

I will harness nature's energy by...

....................................................................................

....................................................................................

....................................................................................